Stay Safe!

Road Safety

Sue Barraclough

Heinemann Library
Chicago, Illinois

© 2008 Heinemann Library
a division of Reed Elsevier Inc.
Chicago, Illinois

Customer Service 888-454-2279
Visit our website at www.heinemannraintree.com

Illustrated by Paula Knight
Designed by Joanna Hinton-Malivoire
Picture research by Erica Martin
Printed and bound in China by South China Printing Co. Ltd.
12 11 10 09 08
10 9 8 7 6 5 4 3 2 1

ISBN 10-digit: 1-4034-9853-9 (hc) 1-4034-9860-1 (pb)

The Library of Congress has cataloged the first edition of this book as follows:
Barraclough, Sue.
  Road safety / Sue Barraclough.
    p. cm. -- (Stay safe)
  Includes bibliographical references and index.
  ISBN-13: 978-1-4034-9853-3 (hc)
  ISBN-13: 978-1-4034-9860-1 (pb)
 1. Traffic safety--Juvenile literature. 2. Pedestrians--Safety measures--Juvenile literature. I. Title.
  HE5614.B34 2008
  613.6'8--dc22
                           2007016384

Contents

Roads are busy places.

Do you know how to stay safe near roads?

Never run into a road.

Do you know how to stay safe near roads?

Never run into a road.

Always stop at the curb.

Never cross a road without looking.

Always look both ways.

Never cross a road near a hill.

Always make sure you can be seen.

Never cross by parked cars.

Always cross at a crosswalk.

Never cross busy roads.

Always use a bridge or tunnel.

Never run ahead.

Always hold hands as you cross.

Never play near a road.

Always find a safe place to play.

Always remember these safety rules.

Always stay safe near roads.

Road Safety Rules

- Stop at the curb before crossing a road.

- Use a crosswalk to cross.

- Look both ways before you cross.

- Listen for cars before you cross.

- Make sure people can see you.

- Use bridges or tunnels if you can.

- Hold hands as you cross the road.

- Find a safe place to play.

Picture Glossary

 **bridge** a path that goes over a road

 **crosswalk** a place on the road where people can cross. Crosswalks may have special colors or lights.

 **curb** the edge of the pavement

 **tunnel** a path that goes under a road so that you can get to the other side

Index

Note to Parents and Teachers

Books in this series teach children basic safety tips for common situations they may face. Discuss road safety with children. Ask them to study the illustrations in the book and think about whether the behavior shown is safe or dangerous. You can ask the class to think of other road safety rules and create a list for the class.

The text has been chosen with the advice of a literacy expert to ensure beginning readers success when reading independently or with moderate support.

You can support children's nonfiction literacy skills by helping students use the table of contents, picture glossary, and index.